GET A G.R.I.P. ON REMOTE WORK

ANDREW W. SILBERMAN

ALSO BY ANDREW W. SILBERMAN

Get a G.R.I.P. - Andrew's Ax Guide to Global Readiness ®
First edition, March 2012. Second edition, July 2017.

Get a G.R.I.P. on Presentations - Andrew's Ax Semi-Secret Guide on What to Say and How to Say It, First edition, September 2019.

TESTIMONIALS

Refreshing to read. Packed full of ideas and tips and all done in the 'best possible taste' (Kenny Everett, British comedian from the late 1970s). Andrew manages to help and develop us without us really feeling any pain. It's his use of music references, self-deprecation, humor, variety and concise method that draws us in and before you know it, it's over. In fact, I was quite looking forward to chapter 11. Being a cricketer there always need to be a number 11!

I passed it to my hugely talented and well-read work colleague (sorry A, I didn't get your permission). She said it was great fun and had such a unique and different approach than other self-help books.

So, thank you Andrew for educating us all on a very topical subject - getting a GRIP ahead of time - it's a must read for all workers!

—*Angus MacGregor, International Head of HR for MUFG*

Securities and Deputy General Manager, Global HR MUFG (Mitsubishi UFJ Financial Group, the world's 5th largest bank by total assets)

This witty and timely book tells us how to deal with the stress Elephant in the room that we don't discuss as much as we should: daily telework, teleconferencing, and scrambling to find the Whatever Button. I am really glad someone who thinks as clearly about communication between human beings as Andrew has offered practical ideas for dealing with the issues that technology imposes, and maybe even find ways to avoid "Zoomicide."

I think this book should be read by anyone working these days, including by participants in our director training courses, where Andrew's lecture on "making a positive impact at board meetings" has been a mainstay for eight years. While slow on the uptake, I've come to see his part of our training as truly essential—for *myself*, as I sit on boards! And now, with remote meetings, making a positive impact has become even more necessary.

Give it to your employees.

—Nicholas Benes, Founding CEO, The Board Director Training Institute of Japan

Many people casually toss the word "insight" around as a cool, catch-all phrase for having understanding. However, I believe it's a blend of Experience and

Context, combined with New Information. Nobody embodies this more than Andrew. His latest book, *Get a G.R.I.P. on Remote Work* is obviously very relevant and well-timed, but also segues brilliantly with his previous super-resourceful books on Global Readiness and Presentations - both of which we discussed when Andrew was a guest on the *Now and Zen* Podcast. The world of work is changing exponentially - WFH, flex-time, shared work stations, etc. Nobody really knows how the new corporate environment will evolve. However, Andrew's book masterfully brings into perspective the challenges and opportunities facing everyone at every level of the organization. And for me, this was indeed a very current and insightful read.

—*Andrew Hankinson, Senior Managing Director, Zwilling J.A. Henckels Japan Ltd.*

INTRODUCTION

First things first.

"Who am I? Why am I here?" Those two questions can set the stage for personal growth or, as Vice Admiral James Stockdale learned in 1992, they can knock you off the public stage for good. Stockdale was Ross Perot's running mate in that year's U.S. presidential election. While their ticket garnered 19% of the popular vote, Stockdale's opening (quoted above) at the vice-presidential debate pretty much doomed him, as it was taken by the snickering audience and the media to mean Stockdale really didn't know who he was, or why he was there. Not the best self-introduction for the candidate's debate.

For our purpose here, my answers to "Who am I?" and "Why am I here?" are simple: I'm someone like you, if you're working remotely at least part of the time. You're on Zoom, Teams, or another video meeting platform and you're combining synchronous (i.e. real-time interactions) and asynchronous (some call "off-line") work. You might be a teacher or student/participant in seminars. Or a manager. In any case, you're attending web-based meetings and managing projects and people in this "new normal" accelerated by the Novel Coronavirus. And you're probably playing family roles too. Like you, I'm doing all the above.

Or better to say, I'm "*trying* to do all the above." Normally I avoid the word "try," taking seriously Yoda's admonition: "Do or do not. There is no 'try.'" But these are far from normal times. Most of us "working from home" are more accurately "trying to work from home while simultaneously adapting to ever-changing social and governmental norms created by COVID-19 fears." At least that's what we're doing in the summer of 2020.

My aim is to inspire new behaviors in order to work more effectively and efficiently right now, and I'll do so by sharing tips, tales, and techniques that can apply well into the future.

And while I'm no technophobe, I'm not a techno*phile* either. Call me "technoskeptical." Like you, I wish I bought as much Apple stock along with each Apple purchase, beginning for me with a Macintosh LC in 1991 and then their first iPod 10 years later. A thousand gadgets later, if accompanied with equal investments in AAPL, just think how rich we would be. But then again, I might not be writing this book, or perhaps I'd be writing it on my own island somewhere near Richard Branson's.

Billionaire neighborhood pipe dreams aside, I'm

still President & Chief Enthusiast for Advanced Management Training Group, K.K. (AMT Group), a company I co-founded in Tokyo back in 1992. For the first five years, I was Director of Graduate School Preparation Services, and the closest thing to "online" work was when my clients would fax me their essays for review. Counseling over 1,000 business school candidates, and having previously served as an Admissions Recruiter/Coordinator for Hawaii Pacific College (now Hawaii Pacific University), perhaps it's no wonder that in addition to AMT Group, I'm also currently teaching in four programs at three universities: Temple University Japan (Masters in Management), Keio University (Global Passport), and Hitotsubashi University (MBA and Executive MBA).

For now, 90% of my interactive work, both for AMT Group and for the universities, is online. As a line from my parody song "Quarantinativille" says, "I tried a new workout. I logged in and Zoomed out." Many of you have been (or are still) there: Zoom fatigue, unwanted COVID-19 pounds...or even kilos, struggling to find anything resembling work/life/school balance, for yourself and for your family members. If so, this book is for you. You can also use it as a diversion, enjoying my and others' online misadventures.

Like you, I've had my fill of frustrations that accompany working remotely. Yet, I've also enjoyed some excellent interactions and completed projects that would have taken much more time and effort, or perhaps would not even have gotten done at all, if not for modern technology that's making remote work possible. If any of this resonates, then, again, this book's for you. For us.

When the pandemic hit, I began chronicling some of the challenges in my blog: "Andrew's Ax," the version of a newsletter I published over 20 years ago. I've compiled those posts and organized them here in an unusual if not unique way for a business book: You can dive into any of the ten chapters, get a quick tip with the two-minute read, and then, enjoy your next virtual meeting or assignment more. Or, you can read the longer, four-minute versions of each chapter. Or get even *more* out of the book by reading both A) and B) versions of a given chapter—the "four-minute" and the "two-minute" reads. Why two versions of each chapter?

They're here to highlight the most important take-away from my experiences with remote work: the value of being concise. As Strunk and White said over 100 years ago, "Vigorous writing is concise. A sentence should contain no unnecessary words, a paragraph no unnecessary sentences, for the same reason that a drawing should have no unnecessary lines and a machine no unnecessary parts."

How many e-mails have you read in the past week that had "no unnecessary words"? If you're like me, more than one. In fact, I bet you received several e-mails that didn't need to be written at all.

At the same time, some people like more details, so I've left in the longer, lightly-edited four-minute versions. This is for readers who want those details, an additional illustration, or who just want to compare the two versions and see for themselves the results of the editing process. I know at least one university professor who uses my blog for this very purpose.

A third reason to read both versions is summed up best by motivational speaker Tony Robbins: "Repetition is the mother of skill." By reading about the same topic twice, and especially when the second version is more concise, my hope is that more of the wisdom shared by others will find a permanent home in us.

I've also added "Cool-down notes" to the end of each chapter. These are my thoughts on the editing process or an additional take on the topic, or an extra word of encouragement. That way, students of concision can see more of the thought process and decision-making that goes into editing.

Cool-down notes were inspired by John Steinbeck's *Journal of a Novel: The East of Eden Letters*. In that insightful book, we read personal letters Steinbeck wrote to his friend and publisher, Pascal Covici. The letters served as a warm-up to the work he was doing on *East of Eden*, one of my favorite novels. Here, my notes will be part of the "cool-down," which any athlete knows is just as important as the warm-up.

REMOTE

T his chapter sets the stage, the starting point on how to "Get A G.R.I.P." on remote work. What do we mean by "remote work"? How can we prepare our work space, our schedule, and other setting issues to make for a better remote work experience? What can we do about the inevitable stress that these changes are bringing? Take a four-minute dive or skip to the two-minute dash.

1A. REMOTE (4-MIN read)

A BEAUTIFUL DOUBLE-MEANING WORD, "REMOTE" can mean, among other definitions, "far away, removed," as when we refer to a remote island, or it could mean that device you use to turn on your TV—you know, the one that can hide itself, sometimes in a remote part of your home! We usually want our remotes close by, not remote!

Today, let's take an intimate look at working remotely. Now that much of the industrialized world is working from home, I want you to avoid falling prey to the prediction Tom Peters made over 25 years ago, when he wrote, in effect, "Digitization will be a professional dream and a personal nightmare." Yes, it's now possible to work from just about anywhere, but how effective will you be from home?

Let's get into it with three main topics: Setting, Scheduling, and Streamlining (or is it going to be "Slacking?")

SETTING

EVERY STAGE PLAY starts out with the "Setting." This often includes both the physical setting, (i.e., "Where is this taking place?" "What items can the audience see when the curtain goes up?") as well as some intangibles ("Where are we in history?" "What is the emotional tenor?"). When it comes to working remotely, I'd like to begin with the latter: What is your predisposition to working from home? Do you have a visceral positive or negative feeling towards it? How is your current set-up at home? Is it conducive to work? Do you have (or can you create) a dedicated space that you use exclusively, or nearly exclusively, for work?

I'm writing this on an old laptop. I don't use this laptop for other purposes. I don't access email on it, don't surf the internet, don't read the news. It's in another part of the apartment (actually, just the other side of my bedroom), so I am training myself to know: "When you sit down at this table, with this laptop, it's time to write. To create. Slacking is done elsewhere."

Back to that question about your feelings toward remote work. I ask because for some people, working from home is a godsend...an escape from the bustling office and its constant interruptions. But as the Spanish saying goes, "The best part of the sunshine is the shade." When there's not even the option of a hustle-and-bustle to escape *from*, remote work can, for some anyway, bring on feelings of loneliness, and you may become less productive. And then there are others who prefer the camaraderie of the office. So review your own values: What is important to you? At least check in on your feelings and thoughts about working from home, as those thoughts can affect the type of setting you want to create.

SCHEDULING

ONE OF MY favorite business writers is Dan Pink. Author of *Drive*, an excellent book on what really motivates us, he then wrote *When* in 2018. In *When*, Pink expounds on the importance of timing. Most important for home working is to find out your own *chrono-type*. Are you naturally an early bird, a night owl, or what he calls a *third bird*, someone who is most alert in the middle of the day (quite rare)? Once you know your chronotype, you can set (and stick to!) a work schedule that makes the most sense for you and the most dollars, yen or euros for your company. Pink's work is worth reading, and finding out your *chronotype* is a straight-forward exercise. You'll also find what kind of work you do at the best time of day to do it.

STREAMLINING or Slacking

I HAVE a client who says that if he can get five solid, focused hours of work from his staff it's a big win. And, he adds, almost no one can actually put in five solid, focused hours in a given work day. From home, you just might be able to. Ask yourself if the activity you are engaged in truly contributes to the bottom line. "The bottom line" is an expression, and it comes directly from accounting—the bottom line of the Income Statement: the document that tallies up all a company's or a division's revenues, subtracts all its expenses, and leaves you with "the bottom line." The answer to the question, "Is this activity truly contributing positively to the bottom line?" may lead you to cut a lot of busywork out of your workday.

.   .   .

STRESS

STRESS IS a topic worthy of a whole book (and some good ones are out there), but I want to touch on it just briefly. If you have gone through a "What's important to me" exercise, and if you're like me and most other people, "health" will come near the top of your list of priorities. With so many working (and some shuttered) at home, physical and psychological health can take a hit. I am making sure to get exercise (a good book to check out is *Your Body Is Your Gym by* Peter Paulson), I meditate twice a day, practice Qigong, and connect with friends and family, but not during those 5–6 hours of focused work.

The odds of this situation lasting for several days or even weeks are not "remote," so let's learn and implement a few practices and get along the best we can. "When the world gives you lemons, make lemonade" sounds good, and it can work—as long as you've got water and sugar to add to the lemons.

1B. REMOTE (2-MIN)

Remote:
1) far away, removed, as a remote island;
2) a TV control device that sometimes hides itself.

WITH SO MANY working from home, how can we avoid Tom Peters' prediction from decades ago: "Digitization will be a professional dream and a personal nightmare"?

SETTING

WRITTEN PLAYS START WITH "SETTING." Setting includes the physical (i.e., "Where's this taking place?" "What does the audience see when the curtain goes up?") as well as intangibles ("What's the mood?"). Let's begin here: Do you have positive or negative feelings towards working at home? How is your current set-up? Can you create a space that you use exclusively for work?

I'm now writing on an old laptop. I don't use this laptop to check e-mail, I don't surf the 'net, or read the news on it. Zero notifications. I work in a small corner of my bedroom. Why? I am training myself: "When you sit down at this table, with this laptop, it's time to write. To create."

For some, working from home is a godsend, an escape from office interruptions. But recall the Spanish saying, "The best part of the sunshine is the shade." When there's no hustle-and-bustle to escape *from* or get back *to*, remote work can increase loneliness and lower productivity. And many prefer the camaraderie of the office. What's important to you? Check in on your views about working from home, as they can affect the setting you want to create. Be aware of your own thoughts and feelings, your preferences.

SCHEDULING

ONE OF MY favorite business writers is Dan Pink. In his 2018 book *When: The Scientific Secrets of Perfect Timing*, he suggests we discover our *chronotype*. Are you an *early bird*, a *night owl*, or what he calls a *third bird*, someone who's most alert in the middle of the day? Once you know your chronotype, set a schedule that makes the most sense for you. Here's a CNBC article that summarizes Pink's main points and helps you discover what to work on and, as his title says, "*When.*"

STREAMLINING or Slacking

ONE OF MY clients asks his staff for five solid, focused hours of work per day. And, he adds, "Almost no one can actually do that." From home, you just might be able to. Ask yourself if the activity you are engaged in truly adds to the bottom line. By "bottom line," I mean the last line of the Income Statement, where a company or division tallies up revenues and subtracts expenses, leaving "the bottom line." You may find it easier than you think to cut out some of what you've been doing.

STRESS

IF YOU HAVE DONE a "What's important to me" exercise, I bet "health" sits at or near the top of your priority list. With so many working (or shuttered) at home, physical and psychological health can take a hit. I am making sure to exercise (a good book to check out is *Your Body Is Your Gym by* Peter Paulson)—I also meditate twice a day and practice Qigong. And I connect with friends and distant family, scheduled *around* (not *during*) those 5–6 hours of focused work.

CHAPTER 1 COOL-DOWN NOTES (For those who read the four- and two-minute versions)

DID the two-minute version leave out anything essential? I don't think so. Here's a little of my editing process, beginning at the end: When I finished reading the four-minute version, I thought, "What's that about lemonade?" It was a little confusing, so that was the easiest line to cut. Especially easy to cut "sugar" since we all want to cut down on sugar. What was I thinking with that last line? I also cut out Dan Pink's first book, which added nothing to the discussion.

Instead, I concluded with some practical advice packaged as something I do myself. I learned a few years ago from podcaster James Altucher that "giving advice never works." First of all, most people don't take it—and secondly, it's arrogant to suggest I have the answer. But I do have suggestions and can share what I do. You might notice I also did my best in the second version to replace longer words with shorter, easier-to-read ones. For example, "What is the emotional tenor?" became "What's the mood?" "Visceral"? "Predisposition"? Cut them out!

DISTRACT

The single biggest issue cited by people who start working remotely is "how to deal with distractions." In this chapter, I share the cry of a professional video editor and give an example of my own, very distraction-prone personality. Do you get distracted while trying to work from home? If so, this chapter's for you!

2A. DISTRACT (4-MIN)

THE ODDS that remote work will last several days, weeks, or even months are not "remote." So like Eric Clapton pleaded in his song *Layla*, "Make the best of the situation, before I finally go insane."

Vocabulary.com defines **distraction** as "something that takes your attention away from what you're supposed to be doing. ... **Distraction** comes from the Latin *dis-*, 'apart,' and *trahere*, 'drag.' So **distraction** is when you're dragged away from your task or from your worries."

Distractions can be a real drag!

In response to my most recent blog, a reader commented, "If working at home was completely without distractions (e.g., wife and child), I could easily start most days super early and be finished with work by lunchtime. That would be a very ideal situation."

I promised that reader to address distraction, and I will. But first, a true story: As many *Ax* Readers know, last year I made a change. I'm still writing blogs and posting them on the AMT Group website, but now I'm following up and sending to a wider audience: "Re-writes," where I take the original 3–4-minute post and cut it down to a 2-minute read. Hence, this *Distract* is supposed to be the first draft. But it's actually the second draft because—get this—I got interrupted, *distracted,* and when I came back to publish, I accidentally overwrote all the text with an image and now am starting anew. I am an expert at "Getting Distracted." And at starting from scratch.

You see, as an ENFP (Myers-Briggs Type Extrovert/iNtuitive/Feeling/Perceiving) the "MBTI prayer" for my type is, "Lord, please give me the power to focus on one thing at a ti—HEY! Look at that bird over there!" Now to be fair (or positively biased) to myself, the distraction today was a most welcome video conference "check-in" call I overheard in the living room—a call between my son and his high school dorm's Residential Faculty (RF). An RF is just like a university dorm's Residence Assistant (RA)—but whereas an RA is an upperclassman, RFs are paid staff. I couldn't help but hear them chatting, and wanted to touch base myself, and then when my brother Blaze and sister-in-law Alyssa joined the call from shuttered-in-place California, I was hooked for nearly an hour.

During and after that hour, I realized a few things about distractions:

1) Distractions are in the eye of the distracted. If something "drags me away from my worries," I thank that something. I would rather do almost anything than "worry." As a previous *Ax* Reader wrote, "Concern is good. Worry not so much." Plus, in this case, that call, which was my "distraction," was the RFs work! It's not the activity (video conference), but the person who decides what is and what is not a "distraction."

2) I can do something about that call and other "distractions." The call wound up being over two hours. For about 1/2 of their call, I came back to my workspace, put in a pair of earplugs, and got to work. (It was a really good draft I lost. Damn.) I also could have chosen Airpods instead of earplugs, and listened to music, but that only works for me if I choose classical music. Otherwise, I'm one of those who's likely to be distracted (I find myself humming or singing along) than letting it be the white noise that works for many others.

3) I recalled my university days. Some of my best

learning was done in the stacks of UC Berkeley's libraries, when I was supposed to be researching one topic but would stumble on, for example, a dedicated copy of Karl Marx's *Das Kapital* and spent an hour combing over its pages. That kind of thing happened more than once, I promise.

4) I learned from Blaze that due to his torn Achilles last year, he's extremely adept at working from home. We discussed several strategies that will show up in future blogs and that can help all of us who are doing much more work from home these days.

There were a couple more learning points but I'm coming up on four minutes and I promised to address the reader who said his life would be ideal if it weren't for his wife and child. Just kidding! I know he didn't mean it that way, even though I first took his comment *almost* that way. (Not as bad as the couple friends I have who say that "business would be perfect if it weren't for employees and customers.")

So "To R.S." (still basically protecting your guilt or innocence by hiding your full name): If indeed you could get your work done by noon if it weren't for your family distracting you (and I agree you could!), here are a couple of things to try out: 1) Let them know your "focused" work schedule, and limit that to 45 minutes per hour. They can interrupt you all they want during the other 15 minutes. This assumes you have at least a small space from which you can work. AMT Group's office for its first year and a half was a futon storage closet in Nakano. Even a closet can work. 2) Wake up

2–3 hours earlier than you normally do, and work while they are asleep. This may sound extreme, and you might wind up going to bed a lot earlier or taking a nap during the day, but how much more productive might you be in the early hours? Then you really *would* be done by noon (or even earlier). 3) Make a list of 10 ways to limit your distractions. Test your favorite one or two for a week. You *will* find a way to limit their distractions. And remember, you're working to support them, right? Maybe work is the distraction and your family the main task? Just a thought.

That's it for now. It was of course a drag when I lost that first draft, but it's happened before and just like that time years ago, the second draft came out much quicker than the first, and I like it more. I hope you do too.

2B. DISTRACT (2-MIN)

VOCABULARY.COM DEFINES **distraction** as "something that takes your attention away from what you're supposed to be doing. ... **Distraction** comes from the Latin *dis-*, 'apart,' and *trahere*, 'drag.' So **distraction** is when you're dragged away from your task or from your worries."

A professional video editor commented on my blog: "If working at home was completely without distractions (e.g., wife and child), I could easily start most days super early and be finished with work by lunchtime. That would be a very ideal situation."

So let's address distraction today. I am an expert at getting distracted. As an **ENFP** (Myers-Briggs Type **E**xtrovert/i**N**tuitive/**F**eeling/**P**erceiving) my "MBTI prayer" is, "Lord, give me the power to focus on one thi —HEY! Look at that bird over there!"

Just yesterday, a video conference taking place in my living room drew me away from my work. Afterward, I reflected on distractions:

1) Distractions are in the eye of the distracted. That call, my "distraction," was my son's Residential Faculty's work. She's in California, calling international students to see how they are coping with this new reality. It's not the *activity* (video-conference), but the *person* who decides what is and what is not a "distraction."

2) I can do something about that call and other distractions. The call lasted over two hours. For 1/2 the time, I was back at my workspace, earplugs in place. I also could have put on some classical or other non-distracting music.

3) As a student, some of my best learning was done in the stacks of UC-Berkeley's libraries. I was supposed to be researching one topic but would stumble on, for example, a dedicated copy of Karl Marx's *Das Kapital* and spend an hour perusing its pages. Distraction led to learning.

4) I learned from my brother Blaze (also on the call yesterday) that due to his torn Achilles last year, he's

become adept at working from home. We discussed strategies that will show up in future blogs (and now this book) that can help all of us who are working remotely.

Back to our distracted video editor: If you could get your work done by noon if it weren't for your family distracting you, here are three potential suggestions: 1) Create and share your focused work schedule, kept to 45 or 50 minutes per hour. Family can interrupt all they want during the other 10-15 minutes. Go interrupt them! 2) Wake up 2 hours earlier than you normally do, and work while they're asleep. This may sound extreme, and you'll wind up going to bed earlier, but how much more productive might you be in the wee hours? And you really would be done by noon. 3) Make a list of 10 ways to limit distractions. Test your favorite one for a week. Repeat. Keep those that work. You *will* find ways to limit their distractions.

One more thought: Maybe work is the distraction and your family the main task. That video conference, that "distraction" was a highlight of my day. And while this might not be the "ideal situation," limiting and dealing with distractions could bring us a step or two closer to it.

CHAPTER 2 COOL DOWN NOTES

AGAIN, WAS ANYTHING SUBSTANTIAL "LOST" between the

versions? Now, it did take me about an hour to cut the total content in half. Concise writing is harder than the initial throwing thoughts down onto a screen. But our job as writers is to make our writing easy to follow and easy to remember. This takes some editing. For this chapter, I cut the part about "re-writes," since the reader either already knows that's what I'm doing (as you do), or in all likelihood, doesn't care about that anyway. I kept the anecdotes because they illustrate what can happen with "good" and "bad" distractions. And I shared a couple of hints and "prove" that one *can* limit distractions, if one chooses.

CLARIFY

A common complaint about remote work is that one or the other party to a communication isn't "clear." A few years ago, Amazon banned the use of pronouns in internal documents. Not in response to the number of genders (now up over 30 in New York City!), but due to confusion over just who is "they" or "we" in a given memo. Now that you're working more remotely, you've got to raise your clarity game up a notch, whether it's during video meetings, e-mail or text, or, as you'll read here, about making a video for others to view asynchronously.

3A. CLARIFY (4-min)

"I want you to want me." Rick Nielson, performed by Cheap Trick

. . .

ACCORDING TO MEDIUM.COM, a 15th century Venetian monk named Angelo Barovier "took seaweed, mixed this with molten glass and formed *cristallo,* the clearest glass anyone had ever seen. He was the first glass maker that produced clear glass." Prior to that time, glass was far from clear. Stained glass is beautiful, but doesn't let in much light. It's a *lot* harder to make clear glass.

The same goes for writing, or indeed any kind of communication. It's easier to be colorful (note how many of today's comedians use "colorful" language to get a laugh) than it is to be clear. So let's take a dive into clarity. Why? Because one of the main reasons that "you can't always get what you want" is that we aren't clear about what we want in the first place.

Case in point: A friend was recording a recruitment video. After slogging through three minutes, you'd be hard-pressed to know exactly what he was hoping to be the outcome of the video. When I asked him about it, he said, "Well, I had eight points I wanted to make." Yes, and your audience, whether they be a viewers of your video, readers of your e-mail, or participants in a meeting, all have very limited attention spans. You may want to communicate eight points, but if even *you* had a hard time remembering them (as any viewer could notice, my friend was checking his notes often), how in the world would the audience remember them? And how clear were you?

Instead, I suggested that for his next video, he get clear, and I mean "*cristallo* clear," on what he wants as a result of his video. Choose one overarching clear goal. Something like, "I want excellent candidates to feel attracted to my company." In another case, you might want "my company to loosen up the 'at desk' rules implemented under the new work-from-home policy." Whatever it is, be clear. There's a reason "Clear" is one of the 7 Cs of Effective Business Writing. It's also one of the most common of the 7 that are forgotten or simply overlooked.

THE EYES HAVE IT

"I WAS BEING CLEAR. They just didn't understand." I have heard that more than once. But communication is a two-way street. If your audience does not "get" your message, the burden rests with you, the sender of the message. Clarify yourself. In person, we get clues from our listeners with micro nods of the head, and also with verbal clues like, "uh-huh," both of which can be missing in the virtual environment.

One of the biggest challenges with Zoom meetings is that you must choose between A) showing eye-contact by looking directly into your camera or B) looking at your audience on your screen. As of today, I don't know of the technology that lets you do both at the same time, which robs us of a key part of in-person communication. We'll be getting more into those and other elements of Zoom/WebEx/BlueJeans meetings in future chapters.

Clarity of expression requires clarity of thought. Rudolf Flesch first wrote *How to Write, Speak and Think More Effectively* in 1946, and yet, except for some of the then-popular references, his book still lives up to its subtitle: "Your complete course in the art of communication." And get this: one of his recommended exercises is to "Write a 500-word essay to a friend every day." Did ol' Rudolf predict blogging?

Not directly. After all, the personal computer was 30+ years away and the internet another couple of decades, but he sure knew his stuff. And he opened my eyes yet again upon re-reading his classic work. Toward the end of a chapter he calls "Freedom from Error," he writes, "Of course we all pride ourselves on having an open mind. But what do we mean by that? More often than not, an open mind means we stick to our opinions and let other people have theirs. This fills us with a pleasant sense of tolerance and lack of bias–*but it isn't good enough*. What we need is not so much an open mind–readiness to accept new ideas–but an attitude of distrust toward *our own ideas*."

We may not all be as crystal clear as to what we want as Rick Nielson was in the song lyric that opens this chapter, but we *can* think through and express what we want before Zooming into our next meeting, e-mail, or video. Right?

. . .

3B. CLARIFY (2-min)

"I want *you* to want *me*." Rick Nielson, performed by Cheap Trick

ACCORDING TO MEDIUM.COM, a 15th century Venitian monk named Angelo Barovier "took seaweed, mixed this with molten glass and formed *cristallo,* the clearest glass anyone had ever seen." Until then, glass was not clear. Stained glass is beautiful, but doesn't let in much light.

The same goes for writing and any communication. It's easier to be colorful than it is to be clear.

CASE IN POINT

A FRIEND POSTED A RECRUITMENT VIDEO. After watching 3 minutes, I hadn't a clue what he was hoping to achieve. "Well, I had 8 points I wanted to make." Yes, and his audience, like yours, is pressed for time. You may *want* to communicate 8 points, but if *you* struggled to remember them (viewers could see my friend checking his notes), how in the world would the *audience* remember them?

I suggested he get clear, and I mean *cristallo* clear, on what he wants as a *result* of his video. Something like, "I want excellent candidates to feel attracted to my company." Or, as with another real case, you might want "my company to loosen up the 'at desk' rules under the new work-from-home policy." Whatever it is, be clear.

THE EYES HAVE It

"I WAS BEING CLEAR. They just didn't understand." How often have you heard that one? If your audience doesn't get your message, the burden rests with *you*, the sender. In person, we get clues from our listeners with micro nods of the head and with verbal clues like, "uh-huh," both of which can be missing in video conferences.

One of the biggest challenges with Zoom meetings is choosing between A) showing eye-contact by looking directly into your camera or B) seeing your audience, by looking at *them*. As of today, I don't know of a technology that lets you do both at the same time. Thus, we're robbed of a key communication clue. This means we need to use polling, "hand raises," and *pauses* more than ever.

Clarity of expression requires clarity of thought. Rudolf Flesch wrote *How to Write, Speak and Think More Effectively* in 1946, and yet his book still lives up to its subtitle: "Your complete course in the art of communication." He shares one of his goals: Raising our respect for rational thought.

Toward the end of a chapter he calls "Freedom from Error?" he writes, "Of course we all pride ourselves on having an open mind. But what do we mean by that? More often than not, an open mind means we stick to our opinions and let other people have theirs. This fills us with a pleasant sense of tolerance and lack of bias—*but it isn't good enough*. What we need is not so much an open mind—readiness to accept new ideas—but an attitude of distrust toward *our own ideas*."

We may only sometimes be as clear as to what we want as Rick Nielson was in "I Want You to Want Me," or Rudolph Flesch above, but we *can* always think through and express what we want before Zooming into our next meeting, right?

CHAPTER 3 COOL-DOWN NOTES

ONE WAY TO check your clarity is to have a smart teenager review your communication. Can they understand it? If so, you're probably being clear enough. Another is to set the writing or video aside for a couple of hours and then check it again for clarity.

Here's an update note on where to put your eyes on a Zoom call. One trick I found takes a little explaining. As I wrote above, we are forced to choose between looking into the camera, which gives anyone on your video call the impression that you are looking at them directly, or you can look at your screen, which lets you see the people on the call. You can't have both, right?

Wrong! It's not a perfect trick, but, if you place a webcam in the middle of your screen, then then you actually can look directly at the person and into the camera at the same time. Instead of using your computer's built-in camera, check out a Logitech webcam (less than $100). Position the camera in the middle of your monitor. The camera is not visible to the participants. When I'm using a large monitor, I put the webcam on a tripod and position it right in the center of my monitor. The camera only blocks a small part of my screen. Now I can look directly in the faces of the people speaking and match the impression given them—that I am looking directly into their eyes.

Again, it's not a perfect trick, but every little bit helps.

One more tiny editing note: I added italics in the Rick Nelson quote to begin the chapter. If you listen to the live version of the Cheap Trick song, you can hear him clearly emphasize, "I want *you* to want *me*." With italics, you can help your readers "hear" which words you want to emphasize.

ZOOM IN!

In this chapter we focus on web meetings, based partly on a conversation I had with the Head of International for Zoom. Most of what we talked about and that I introduce here can be used across any of the web-based meeting platforms.

4A. ZOOM IN! (4-min)

ONE FAVORITE LINE in the original "Wayne's World" Saturday Night Live sketches and movies is, "Unnecessary Zoom!" Today, that phrase takes on a new meaning if you, like so many professionals, have had your life enhanced (and consumed) by video conferences.

In the late spring of 2020, I met Abe Smith, Head of International for Zoom. Introduced by my brother, I met Abe—how else?—on a Zoom call. He had the Golden Gate Bridge as his background (a Zoom feature), and I really enjoyed our first meeting. He shared his mission: "We're in the business of connecting businesses through video and delivering happiness."

I mentioned that I'm writing on a book to help distributed teams work better together, and I didn't have to tell Abe that a big part of that work is now being done through Zoom. Their sales, along with their stock price, are—pardon the pun—zooming! When I mentioned that I'd be focusing on helping people use Zoom, though, I don't think I was clear enough with my intention. (Didn't I read Chapter 4?) His answer, which anyone who's used Zoom will affirm was, "You don't really need extensive training to use Zoom." — in fact, that's one of the reasons Zoom's founder, Eric Yuan, left Cisco/WebEx. Eric wanted an easier platform, and one that was as stable or better than FaceTime.

Abe's right. Zoom's easy to set up, easy (and even fun) to use, but...yes, there's a "but" that follows, and it's not a pretty one. See, it's not about the technology—it's about the people communicating (or better said, *mis*communicating) on Zoom and other video conferencing platforms. Yes, Zoom is easy to use, but a *lot* of people aren't using it well.

I've received complaints (and training requests) due to the lack of skills people are demonstrating while on a video or tele-conference. These skill deficiencies include: lack of preparation; lack of understanding how, when, and why to use mute; sharing vs. hiding video; sharing screens; rushing through poorly presented slides; and a whole host of other issues that all can be summed up under the umbrella of "lack of professional communication skills." We touched last time on the importance of "clarity," why being crystal clear with your communication goals is crucial, and there are several more considerations. We'll hit a few today.

First, there's culture. I just read a non-Japanese share her Japanese colleague's post from a video conference: "I'm Japanese so I'm shy to show my face." True, shyness is considered a virtue in Japanese society, but being the one (or one of very few) people on a video conference to hide your face is probably going to look bad to your global peers.

If you're only joining a meeting to receive information, or if you've agreed to reduce bandwidth by shutting off video, that's one thing—but if you are going to be speaking to the group, and the meeting is called a "video conference," then it's probably best to turn on your camera. And position it to show not your nostrils, or the top of your head, or a ceiling fan, but your upper body. Set up proper lighting. Cut down on echo by using a headset if you're in a large room. As for your shyness, you wouldn't stand outside a meeting room because you're shy, would you? And your company is not paying you to attend the meeting "because you're shy." They want you to "show" up!

Here are some other common complaints I'll share so that no one will be complaining about *you* doing them: Lack of building rapport, just going straight into the content; delivering a presentation (say Power-Point®) and failing to put it into Presentation Mode (therefore the slides are too small to see); failure to ask questions; speakers rarely, if ever, looking into their camera; and one that particularly bothers some: the frantic head-nodding and double-hand waving at the end of the call, as though participants are sending loved ones off on a cruise.

Video-conferencing etiquette is, for many, still in its early stages. We have yet to see many formal norms across industries, companies, or departments. Still, you can go a long way toward better performance by keeping your audience in mind: Speak clearly, and briefly; ask questions; paraphrase; summarize. Ask someone to take notes during the meeting. If you can finish in less time than the meeting has been planned for, end it! And use a survey tool to ask for feedback in order to improve the next meeting. Oh, and by the way, don't look or sound like you just woke up.

A lot of the missteps people are making are the same ones we've seen and heard when it comes to presenting yourself at any kind of meeting. Issues with slides, with clarity, with engagement. It gets a lot harder for most of us to keep paying attention while sitting in front of a screen than it does when we're all seated around the same table. So it's time to ramp up our professional communication skills and apply them (as well as some new skills) to video-conferences.

If we do, then in addition to the necessary Zooms, we'll be able to shout with Garth and Wayne: "Party on! Excellent!"

4B. ZOOM IN! (2-min)

ONE FAVORITE LINE in the "Wayne's World" Saturday Night Live sketches and movies is, "Unnecessary Zoom!" Today, that phrase takes on a new meaning if you have had your life enhanced (and consumed) by video-conferences.

In the spring of 2020, I met Abe Smith, Head of International for Zoom. I met Abe—how else?—on Zoom. I really enjoyed our meeting and love his mission: "We're in the business of connecting businesses through video and delivering happiness." I mentioned that I'm writing a book for distributed teams. When I said I'd be including a section on helping people use Zoom, he said, "You don't really need extensive training to use Zoom." He added it's super-intuitive. That's one of the reasons Zoom's founder, Eric Yuan, left Cisco/WebEx. Eric wanted an easier platform, and one that was as stable or better than FaceTime.

Abe's right. Zoom's easy to set up and easy to use. The problem is not the technology—it's the people communicating (or *mis*communicating) on Zoom and other platforms.

I've received complaints due to the lack of skills people are demonstrating on video conferences. These include: lack of preparation; lack of understanding how and when to mute; rushing through poorly created slides; and a whole host of other issues that all can be summed up under one umbrella: "Lack of professional communication skills." We touched last time on why being clear with your communication goals is crucial, and there are several more considerations.

First, there's culture. "I'm Japanese so I'm shy to show my face." If you've agreed to reduce bandwidth by shutting off your video, that's one thing—but if you're going to be speaking to the group, and the meeting is called a "video conference," then it's best to turn on your camera. And position it to show not your nostrils, or the top of your head, or a ceiling fan. Use good lighting. Cut down on echo by using a headset.

Some other complaints I'll share so no one will be complaining about *you* doing them: Lack of building rapport; delivering a presentation and failing to put it into Presentation Mode; speakers and participants not asking questions or looking into their cameras; and one that particularly bothers some: the frantic head-nodding and double-hand waving at the end of the call, as though participants are sending loved ones off on a month's long cruise.

Video etiquette is still in its early stages. Still, you

can improve performance by keeping your audience in mind: Speak clearly, and briefly; ask questions; paraphrase; summarize. Ask someone to take notes during the meeting, then post them. If you finish in less time than the meeting has been planned for, end it! And survey for feedback in order to improve the next meeting.

A lot of missteps people are making are the same ones we've seen and heard when it comes to presenting yourself at any kind of meeting. Issues with slides, clarity, and engagement. And it's harder to keep paying attention while sitting in front of a screen. So let's ramp up our professional communication skills and apply them to video conferences, and add in some necessary new tech skills too.

If we do, then in addition to the necessary Zooms, we'll be able to shout with Garth and Wayne: "Party on! Excellent!"

CHAPTER 4 COOL-DOWN NOTES

RE-READING this chapter's two versions, I thought I'd accidentally posted the 2-minute version twice. And yet, you can count for yourself: the 4-minute chapter is 902 words and the 2-minute is 550. Thirty-nine percent fewer words and zero loss of the main message. And those two minutes saved are "per person." Multiply those two minutes by the number of people reading, and that's a lot of potential time that can be put to another good use. The same goes for all of your writing. Think of the time you're saving others. Take the time to edit. The time you save your readers belongs to your whole organization.

And as the chapter says, remote work is not *all* about efficiency. We are missing the social cues, the small-talk on the way in and out of meetings, and more when we move to remote work. So take time to establish rapport and check in with your team members before diving into the agenda.

Key chapter take-aways: Set up your technology, camera angles, lighting. Practice good video meeting etiquette, use your communication skills, and most important of all: Show up!

ESSENTIAL READING & A FORGOTTEN SKILL

This was originally a mindset chapter. Rather than look at skills or techniques, we explored "what really matters" and how to stay motivated while working remotely. If you are already self-assured that your work is meaningful, and that you just want to get better at it, then feel free skip this chapter and jump right to the Cool Down Notes, where I've added some thoughts on the "forgotten skill" of listening. (I'm referring to listening as a "forgotten skill," having been strongly influenced by Madelyn Burley-Allen's great book, *Listening: The Forgotten Skill: A Self-Teaching Guide*.)

5A. ESSENTIAL READING (4-min)

MY FRIEND BILL is a financial analyst for an investment

bank. When COVID-19 struck, he says he became busier than ever, working from home, "sheltered in place" in Brooklyn, New York. When his firm published a list of "essential workers," those allowed (or required) to come into the office, his name wasn't on the list. "I get it," Bill said. "I'm not on the trading floor. But still, it was a gut punch; I'm not 'essential.'"

Another friend and former colleague, Eriko, is now an in-house corporate trainer for a major tech company. When about a month ago her firm informed staff of "travel deemed not essential," at the top of their list was "Training." She laughed as she told me, and pointed out that in her case, the reason was that most training could be done over video conference, "But still..." she said.

"But still...." When much of the world went into "lock down," or "shelter-in-place," or whatever other new-phrase-of-the-day put to use, I couldn't help but notice that every local and national government agrees that certain "essential" work must go on: hospitals (of course, this is a health issue first), grocery stores ("we gotta eat!"), fire and police departments are all considered "essential." But what of those who support them? Deliveries, hospital administrators, telephone operators are all "essential," are they not?

I agree they're all doing essential work. So is Eriko. And Bill. Without analysis, traders have only guesswork. Not every service is directly saving lives, but we're all interconnected. And often it's just a question of framing, as I learned from Tom Peters years ago. He was explaining how some services, like hotel house-keeping, might be lower on the "status chart" of a hotel —after all, a hotel is not in the business of housekeeping. But if you run a housekeeping company, "House-keeping" *is* the cores service you provide.

In business, I've learned, "The most important job is often the one that's not getting done." At one point, we were told to "Just stay home," as though binge-watching Netflix and eating chips was our civic duty. Balderdash! There's more to be "done." I'm taking the time to reflect, especially on what's "essential" in my work, in my personal life, and in the world. Who knows where the next great idea is going to come from? It might be yours! I'm also going outside, even if just to my balcony, as much as possible. Physical distance, yes, but under the sun!

Mark Cuban (billionaire, "Shark Tank" star, owner of the Dallas Mavericks) was being interviewed during the early days of the pandemic, and after several inter-esting, thoughtful and thought-provoking observa-tions, he said, "We need the NBA." Now, I've always been a sports fan, and I love the NBA (moreso when the Warriors were winning). What he meant was, as he also said, "We human beings need entertainment." "We need community." But do we *need* the NBA? We need food, but do we "need" every item in the grocery store? As much as we need our WiFi to stay up and running? No WiFi would *really* leave us all in a lurch. Who's planning for that?

Numbers and statistics can boggle the mind. The

U.K.'s *Guardian* projects that the 2020 economic shock could knock 500,000,000 (1/2 a billion) people back from "poor" into destitute-level poverty. It could turn the clock back 30 years. Are those people any less "essential" than the thousands (or even hundreds of thousands) we may (hopefully) have saved by implementing these economic measures? I don't know. Maybe you don't know either. Nobody knows.

But I do know that if you're reading this, you have essential work to do. We all do. It doesn't matter if your position in your company is deemed "essential" by someone else, or if your company or industry is one of the "protected few." To see how capricious such judgements can be, let's compare two industries in California and Japan. Here in Tokyo, hair salons never faced recommendations to reduce hours or to close. In San Francisco, those same salons would be closed or fined for trying to stay open. A bit of a contrast, yes? Here's a bigger one: In San Francisco, cannabis dispensaries are considered by the government to be "essential businesses."

Beyond the work you do, you're "essential" for who you are. It doesn't matter if your work or position has received the "Essential" stamp. If you can't think of anything in particular to do, I suggest studying up on the power of practicing mindfulness and gratitude. There are a lot of tools available. Three of my favorite apps are Calm, 10% Happier, and Waking Up. Great interviews, stories, and exercises in all of them.

Or just listen. On April 12, 2020, Sam Harris (who

offers the Waking Up app) interviewed Laurie Santos, a professor at Yale, on "The Science of Happiness" on Harris's "Making Sense" podcast. Some of the interview is behind a subscriber paywall (but Sam waives fees for anyone under financial stress). I highly recommend that interview as well as the sources quoted in it. Professor Santos has her own podcast, "The Happiness Lab," and was also interviewed by "Choiceology" (from Charles Schwab) in a podcast called "Coronavirus BONUS: Laurie's Personal Tips."

Staying positive isn't always easy, just as "Life isn't always equal" (one of my dad's favorite phrases.) I truly feel for those who have been directly affected by the virus and by the economic shock, as well as for those feeling any and all the frustrations related to the pandemic. My grandfather and father (both surgeons) used to say, "The mortality rate of the human race is 100%." You'd be hardpressed to find a truer fact than that. But while we're living, there's work to be done. After all, we are essentially human beings...and all "Essential."

5B. ESSENTIAL READING (2-min)

BILL IS a financial analyst for an investment bank. During the pandemic, he was busier than ever, working from home in Brooklyn, New York. When his firm published a list of "essential workers," (those allowed to come into the office) his name wasn't on it. "I get it," Bill said. "I'm not on the trading floor. But still, it was a gut punch; I'm not 'essential.'"

When much of the world went into "lock down," or "shelter-in-place," everyone agreed that certain "essential" work must go on: hospitals, grocery stores, fire and police departments—are all considered "essential."

As they clearly are. Now on the flip side, anthropologist David Graeber argues that around 40% of us are engaged in work that doesn't really serve society. On his list: Lobbyists, Corporate Attorneys, Advertisers, and right near the top: HR Consultants. Ouch! His book, *Bullshit Jobs* is compelling, disturbing, and laugh-out-loud funny.

In business I've learned, "The most important job is often the one that's not getting done." At one point, we were told to "Just stay home," and some acted as though binge-watching Netflix was our civic duty. Balderdash! I'm reflecting on what's "essential" in my work, in my personal life, and in the world. I'm also going outside as much as possible.

"The next bright idea could come from any of us," Mark Cuban said in an interview in the early days of the pandemic. The billionaire, "Shark Tank" star, and owner of the Dallas Mavericks also said, "We human beings need entertainment. We need community." Yes, yes! But he also said, "We need the NBA." Ah, no. The NBA is "*fan*tastic" as the ad went, but sorry, Mark, even fans like us know the NBA is not a necessity.

If you're reading this, you have essential work to do, whether or not your position or company is deemed "essential." To see how subjective it is, let's compare two industries in two places. Here in Tokyo, hair salons were not asked to reduce hours, let alone close. In San Francisco, those same salons would be fined for staying open. Quite a contrast. Here's a bigger one: In San Francisco, cannabis dispensaries are considered "essential businesses."

On April 12, 2020, Sam Harris interviewed Laurie Santos, a professor at Yale, on "The Science of Happiness" on his "Making Sense" podcast. Some of the interview is behind a subscriber paywall (Sam waives fees by request). I highly recommend that interview as well as the sources quoted in it. Sam and Laurie are doing essential work and they helped me do mine. They can help you, too.

Staying positive isn't always easy. I feel for all those who have been affected by the virus and by the economic shock, as well as for those feeling any the frustrations related to the pandemic. My grandfather and father (both surgeons) used to say, "The mortality rate of the human race is 100%." But while we're living, there's work to be done. After all, we are essentially human beings...and all "Essential."

CHAPTER 5   COOL-DOWN   NOTES   AND THOUGHTS ON THE FORGOTTEN SKILL

· · ·

THIS CHAPTER WENT under the editing knife more than others. In cutting the four-minute version down to two, I removed two examples and added in another. I chopped the story of my former colleague because I felt it didn't add as much to the article as the quick summary of *Bullshit Jobs*. And I didn't see a reason to touch on COVID-19's devastating impact on the global economy, mainly because I didn't think my time-pressed readers would relate so much to the numbers. It was "nice to have" rather than "need to have." And again, no message loss by cutting the number of words nearly in half.

SOME THOUGHTS on the Forgotten Skill of Listening

MADELYN BURLEY-ALLEN'S book I referenced at the top of this chapter is always worth a read and a re-read, taking the time to go through its self-teaching exercises. More than any other skill, the best communicators possess an extraordinary ability to listen. They listen to themselves, to others, to whole groups. They have developed the knack of changing their tone, vocabulary level, and even content of a given message depending on what they pick up while listening.

But her book was written in 1995, at the dawn of the internet, long before web-based meetings. One of the biggest challenges we face on these meetings is sound: vocal connections are cut, either by an unstable internet or misuse of the mute button. Even the most stable platforms run into problems. What can you do about this? How can we improve our and others' listening while working remotely? Having struggled through too many tough calls, here are my thoughts, presented for you as a Top 5 Things to Remember:

1. Sound issues *will* crop up. Be ready for them. Don't be surprised or express frustration when they do.

2. Use "chat," "polling," or other meeting software add-on apps so you don't need to rely on people listening accurately to you or to anyone else. You may not know when a given person's connection has failed.

3. Assign a note-taker. Consider posting notes "live" in the chat. Participants can ask for clarification or edits along the way. And rotate the note-taker role.

4. Assign or play the role of "summarizer." This person recaps what you've covered every 10 minutes or so. This is *not* a waste of time—it's an investment of time and return on the investment is greater clarity. Alternatively, you could ask everyone to type in their own biggest take away from the meeting. If people know they'll be asked to do so, their listening will *automagically* improve.

5. Model the way by sharing when your

connection has failed, or when you've had trouble hearing someone. Ask the person speaking to repeat what they said or post it in chat.

And don't worry about silence—encourage it! "Zoom fatigue" is a real phenomenon, and it's partly caused by the non-stop voices emanating from small speakers. Allow time for reflection, time that's often missing from in-person meetings. You might be surprised at the better results that come from giving your people more time to think.

You're doing essential work, and one of the most essential elements of your work is to improve your and your team's listening skills.

SCREENED OUT

A deeper dive into what's happening on some web-based meetings, along with some tips to stay motivated and make web meetings better for everyone.

6A. SCREENED OUT (4-min)

"LIVE IS LIFE."
   —Opus (Austrian band), 1985

HOW I MISS THE "LIVE HOUSE" experience! Whether it's up on stage or in the audience, nothing compares to the sensory overload that comes with a packed room, flashing lights, spilled drinks, and Marshall amps blasting at a real live performance. Coming in a distant second place is watching an amazing movie like *Shine a Light, Bohemian Rhapsody, Great Balls of Fire,* or *Ray,* four of my favorites. Or how about a great music video? Just before sitting down to write today, I watched, for the first time, the original video from the quoted song above, "Live is Life." I knew the song packed some kind of punch (Europe's Number 1 in the summer of 1985) but I had no idea how corny the video would be, or how accurate it is in a deeper sense: Live music is transformative.

I turn to the screen for inspiration, and for a break from...the screen?! I watch the new Michael Jordan Netflix documentary, *Last Dance,* then flip over to a shorter one on John Stockton where one of the biggest compliments he gets is that even as a "scrawny" point guard, he was always ready, willing, and able to set a screen on giants like Shaquille O'Neal. "Setting a screen" means to block out a defender so that your teammate can get an open shot. It's a tough move. You can be called for a foul or get seriously injured both in setting and running into a solid screen. In basketball, it's no fun being screened out. And as many of us are finding, it's no fun in business, either: When working remotely we can feel "screened out."

I noticed this after facilitating a New Member Orientation for the American Chamber of Commerce (ACCJ). There was just a handful of us in that particular Zoom session, unlike many video conferences or classes. Still, I felt the frustration level rise and then I reflected on why.

First, while I've conducted hundreds of these orientations in the ACCJ boardroom, this was only my second time attending (and first time leading) a session over Zoom. The previous one I attended was at noon. This one took place from 18:30–19:30. That was one big difference. One participant said she had been on Zoom calls since 7:30 that morning. Oh boy! Interestingly, despite her apology for "losing her voice," she was fully engaged and lifted the energy of the call. I'm super grateful for her presence.

That can't be said for everyone on that or any other call. It's understandable: it was the end of the day, people were tired of being "present" for one more video call of any kind. Prior to COVID-19, those end-of-day interactive presentations had always been a highlight of a given week. But it's one thing to head over the ACCJ, mingle with new members around a buffet, share a cocktail, get into a presentation, meet some great people, and then walk on down to BAUHAUS for some rock music on my way home.

It's quite another to gear up for one more session of what *Psychology Today* calls "high intensity virtual connecting." In an April 4 article, Suzanne Degges-White writes about "Zoom Fatigue" and warns, "Don't Let Video Meetings Zap Your Energy."

Personally, I wish video meetings *would* zap (and not sap) my energy, but that's just a left-over word choice from a short management book I enjoyed years ago, *Zapp! The Lightning of Empowerment*. In that book, William Byham's powerful message is to seek out "energy zappers" and avoid "sappers." Both Deges-White's article and Byham's book share a common theme, and it's the same as Star Trek's command: Energize!

Any given Zoom call can be more enjoyable for *everyone* when we realize that each of our contributions (or non-contributions) makes a difference. We have yet to work out the best etiquette for all video conferences but let me make a couple suggestions based on what I have seen so far.

1) ENGAGE. Whoever is leading a video conference is working harder than they do in person. Just as there's more bandwidth used over the internet for video conferences, the call leader's personal "bandwidth" is being stretched as she or he monitors participants, checks who is muted or not, fusses with slides, videos, or other media, strains to hear clearly, and confirms understanding (demonstrably less than in face-to-face meetings). You can take some of the burden off the leader by engaging positively, asking good questions, and helping drive the call toward its goal.

2) BE CONCISE. Please! I'm going to keep saying this till it gets through. Until 5G gets here, there are no real-time, natural social cues to let you know that you're being long-winded. If you have a tendency to go on too long in a real conversation (and have the self-aware-

ness to know), be aware that a video meeting exaggerates the effect. Some tend to think, "I've got the mic" as if they're at a karaoke party, and they go on for the length of a song, or longer. That's 2–3 minutes too long. A 30-second comment or question is generally the sweet spot.

3) AGAIN, **ENERGIZE!** Energy is contagious. During the pandemic, we're all tired of something. Tired of video-conferences, tired of "shelter-in-place," tired of anxiety, tired of watching the scale go up, or for some, tired of watching it go down. But in a video meeting, you can choose to bring the energy UP. Your tone of voice, your posture (try standing up), your comments, all of these and more can and will make the meeting go better or worse, for yourself and for everyone else.

If you need a break, and have five minutes, stand up, head over to YouTube and search for Opus, "Live is Life" original and live versions.

"LIVE IS LIFE!"

6B. SCREENED OUT (2-min)

"LIVE IS LIFE."
—Opus (Austrian band), 1985

. . .

HOW I MISS THE "LIVE HOUSE." On stage or in the audience, nothing compares to the packed rooms, the Marshall amps, the high fives. Coming in a distant second: Watching the movies *Shine a Light, Bohemian Rhapsody,* or *Ray.* Or a music video. Before editing today, I watched the original Opus music video, *Live is Life*, Europe's Number 1 song in the summer of 1985. A corny video for sure, and accurate too: Live music is transformative.

I turn to the screen for a break from...the screen. In basketball, you set a screen to block out a defender. It's a tough move. You can be called for a foul or get seriously injured setting or running into a screen. It's no fun being screened out in basketball. And it's no fun in business, either: During the pandemic, we're all "screened out."

I noticed this after facilitating a New Member Orientation for the American Chamber of Commerce (ACCJ). There were just a handful of us there, unlike many video meetings. Still, I felt my frustration rise. Why?

First, while I've led hundreds of orientations in the ACCJ boardroom, this was only my second over Zoom. The previous one was over lunch, whereas this one started at 18:30. One member had been on Zoom since 7:30 AM. Despite her apology for "losing her voice," she was fully engaged.

I used to love New Member Orientations. But it's

one thing to breeze over to the ACCJ, mingle with new members, share cocktails, deliver a presentation, and then walk to BAUHAUS and rock out before heading home. Quite another gearing up for one more session of what *Psychology Today* calls "high-intensity virtual connecting."

A video meeting can be more enjoyable for *everyone* when we realize that each of our contributions makes a difference. We have yet to work out the etiquette norms but here are a few suggestions to make your next meeting better:

1) ENGAGE. Meeting leaders are working harder than they do in person. Their "bandwidth" is stretched: monitoring participants, checking who's muted, fussing with slides, straining to hear. You can reduce their burden by engaging positively, asking good questions, and helping drive the call toward its goal.

2) BE CONCISE. Please! Some act as if they've taken the karaoke mic, and they speak for the length of a song. That's three minutes too long. A 30-second comment or question is generally the sweet spot.

3) ENERGIZE! Energy is contagious. These days, we're all tired of something. But in a video meeting, *you* can bring the energy UP. Your tone of voice, your

posture—try standing up!—your comments, all of these can and will make a difference, for yourself and for everyone else.

If you need a break, and you have five minutes, enjoy Opus right now or right before your next video meeting. Go to Youtube and search for Opus, "Live is Life" original and live versions. Watch, listen, sing and dance, right now and before your next video meeting. What have you got to lose but the Screened-out blues?

"LIVE IS LIFE!"

CHAPTER 6 COOL-DOWN NOTES

MY BOOKS HAVE exercises that I recommend you do. And I often suggest songs to listen to. Informal research has led me to conclude that not many readers actually *do* the exercises or take the time to check out the songs. It's understandable—you're in "reading" mode. I get it. But this chapter's song, "Live is Life" and the videos of them, are just too good, too inspiring, too uplifting, to go unwatched. Check them out. If not right now, then when? "Live is Life!"

ACTION!

This is a "meaty" chapter. It covers your set-up, your personal appearance, some blunders that many professionals make, and what you can do and say (and *not* do and *not* say) to make your video meetings go better. For many of us, the heart of collaborative work online is the video conference. So let's go deeper here.

7A. ACTION! (4-min)

"WHAT WE'VE GOT HERE IS a failure to communicate."
Cool Hand Luke

Once upon a time, companies like Disney were outliers, calling their theme park staff "actors." How the tables have turned! The parks are all closed during the pandemic, and like it or not, every professional taking part in video conferences has become an actor. This will be true long after the pandemic subsides.

Some of the most popular YouTube videos in the summer of 2020 focus on lighting, hardware, and software designed to make us look better. In a way, this makes sense, since, according to Albert Mehrabian's oft-quoted research, how you look contributes more toward a positive reception than does either how you sound or what you say. A positive image is created visually.

So it's no wonder many of us want to invest at least some time in how we look before jumping onto our next Zoom meeting. If you haven't already checked out any of those videos, I can save you some time: 1) Set your camera at approximately eye level; 2) ensure you have adequate light in front of you (rather than behind or above); 3) frame yourself so as to be well positioned on the screen, and not too large or too small. If you also care to present a "professional" image, women may want a little (not a lot) more make-up than you wear to work, and men may want to wear a collared shirt rather than a t-shirt or a hoodie. That's all.

And it's not all. There's a lot to be learned before gaining proficiency at leading or presenting during these virtual meetings. Just knowing the difference between a "meeting" and "webinar," for example, seems to be taking time to break through the mind fog of "work from home" professionals.

A "webinar," according to Zoom, is meant for one-to-many presentations. It's like a broadcast—whereas a meeting is meant for interaction. The distinction may be subtle, but the majority of "meetings" I've been attending recently are really webinars with some opportunity for questions if you'll raise your hand. This sometimes sort of works, but it's not ideal. People are lulled to "sleep" much quicker than when in person, unless the speaker is incredibly dynamic and the topic super on target for a particular audience.

This seems to be lost on the average presenter/speaker, and at least as of summer 2020, participants, stuck at home for the most part, are more likely to log in and stay logged in than they will be once they're free to do other things. So unless you're a popular podcaster or DJ who can entertain audiences without an interviewee, I suggest ramping up real interaction. If you have a large group, use the "polling" function. It's engaging, you get real-time responses, and polling gives everyone in your audience something to do other than to sit and watch. Use polling to survey opinions, suss out questions, and if you're really daring, use a poll as a quiz to see if people are actually processing your material accurately.

It's not for the faint of heart. Results of polling reveal just how little communication is taking place.

Or make quick break-out groups. Let people briefly process and discuss what they think "so far" for just three minutes. What's one question they have? Then bring them back. Now have them post their questions in chat. Later put them in pairs. Have them discuss: What surprised them? What are they still wondering about? These take next to no time at all to implement. Let's be creative and come up with new ways to engage, to attract and keep attention, for as long as the meeting goes.

Speaking of which, there's no harm in ending a meeting before the allotted time. I have a friend, a big fan of colorful language, who puts it like this: "With five or 10 minutes till the hour is up, and we've covered everything on the agenda, why is there always some idiot who has to bring up some hypothetical BS topic that's never going to f-ing happen...and I gotta pee!" I hear you, D.M. The one caveat to ending early is if you have promised a Q & A session, and someone has been waiting to ask a question, and then you suddenly end the meeting. Bad move.

We're doing more video conferences than we ever planned on, and just like the movie, they're bringing out "The Good, the Bad, and the Ugly." Speaking of ugly....

Have you heard of the "transcribe" option open to Zoom Enterprise customers? It's great and it's awful. The "transcribe" option fairly accurately records, in text, what people say during a Zoom meeting or webinar. Warning: The system is accurate enough to include all your filler words. One recent speaker said "you know" 15 times in less than two minutes, and

continued apace. If he were to see his comments transcribed, he would likely (and rightfully) be mortified.
Toastmasters, the public speaking organization, knows
this, which is why they assign an "um/ah" counter. At
the end of their meetings, the counter reports how
many filler words were used by meeting participants,
and some members feel rightly embarrassed as they
pay fines for each infraction. How would they feel
seeing their filler words in black and white? Here's an
example:

"Well, you know, the report we have here, you
know, kind of shows how we're ah, you know, still
growing, but, you know, it's not at all clear, that ah, you
know, we'll stay on this positive trajectory." That
painful example is, sadly, not an exaggeration. The
most infamous "you know" video doomed Caroline
Kennedy's run for a Senate seat in 2008. Google it and
gag. There's a two-minute clip that I can listen to for
just 1:00. You're probably not running for Senate, but
we're watching and listening to your "performance" on
a screen just the same.

Andy Bergin (founder of Speaking Virtually)
reminded me to remind you: "It's not the technology
that matters—it's the person *using* the technology that
makes the difference." So in your next action role, that
is, your next video meeting: Be Good, not Bad, not
Ugly!

7B. ACTION! (2-min)

.   .   .

"WHAT WE'VE GOT HERE IS a failure to communicate." *Cool Hand Luke*

Everyone's an actor. Popular YouTubers teach how look better on video. This makes sense, since how you look contributes more toward a positive reception than how you sound or what you say. A quick summary: 1) Set your camera at eye level; 2) source light in front; 3) frame yourself so you won't look too big—or too small.

There's more. Start with the difference between a "meeting" and "webinar." W*ebinars* are "one-to-many presentations." A *meeting* is for interaction. Most "meetings" I've attended are actually webinars with questions tacked onto the end. That works only when the speaker is dynamic and the topic spot on. Unless you're like podcaster Joe Rogan, who can entertain without an interviewee, ramp up interaction. Use the "polling" function. Polling engages and gives something more to do than sit, watch, and listen. Use break-out groups or break-out pairs. Or one then the other. Discuss: What surprised them? What questions do they have?

There are other ways to engage, attract, and keep attention for as long as the meeting goes. Speaking of which, why use all the allotted time? A friend who loves colorful language put it like this: "Really pisses me off! There's five or 10 minutes left. We've covered everything on the agenda. Then there's some f-ing idiot who brings up some hypothetical bullshit topic that's never gonna f-ing happen, and I gotta pee!"

I hear you, D.M. (and here's some soap for your mouth). Just don't end early if you promised Q & A and someone's waiting with question. Let them ask! After answering, end the meeting, but not "end for everyone." Let those who want stay and chat.

Just Like the Movie

We're on video more than ever, and just like the Clint Eastwood movie, we're seeing "The Good, the Bad, and the Ugly."

Speaking of ugly...have you heard of the "transcribe" option? It records, in text, words spoken during a Zoom session. One recent speaker said "you know" 15 times in less than two minutes. If he were to see his comments transcribed, he would be rightfully mortified. Toastmasters assigns an "um/ah" counter, one member who reports filler words used by speakers. Imagine how you would feel if this was your last sentence: "Well, you know, the report we have here, you know, kind of shows how we're ah, you know, still growing, but, you know, it's not at all clear, that um, you know, we'll stay on this positive trajectory."

That painful example is, sadly, *not* an exaggeration. It can be infuriating. The most infamous "you know" video doomed Caroline Kennedy's Senate run.

Google it and gag. Now...you're not running for the Senate, but you are running a meeting. And we're watching.

Andy Bergin (friend, coach, founder of Speaking Virtually) reminded me to remind you: "It's not the technology that matters—it's the person *using* the technology that makes the difference." So in your next action role, that is, your next video meeting: Be Good, not Bad, and not Ugly!

CHAPTER 7 COOL-DOWN NOTES

ONE MORE HINT for appearing better on camera is the judicious use of "concealer" for both men and women. Concealer (I called it "canceller" for the first month or so) removes shininess and redness from your face when lights are directly on you. The key word, especially for those not accustomed to using concealer, is "judicious." Don't cake it on!

One more suggestion for making long-ish video meetings go better: Give people breaks. At least five minutes per hour and 15 minutes at a three-hour mark. Have everyone turn OFF their video cameras, get up, stretch...move! Get their eyes off their monitors. Some may check e-mail or another computer-related task, but I suggest not doing that yourself. Everyone needs real breaks from these high intensity interactions focused on a monitor. What you *don't* do can have an even greater positive effect on your meetings than what you *do* do.

Nick Benes, Chair of the Board Directors Training Institute, points out that looking and sounding confident is even more important over web conferences. Some ways to "look and sound" confident are to *stand up*, ensure you're framed correctly, and speak right into the camera.

CAMERA ON/OFF

Here we'll take a look at a controversial topic, and you'll also enjoy my own foibles when it comes to "performing" during a video meeting. As I wrote in the introduction, I'm "techno-skeptical," and prior to every web session, my anxiety level rises. "What might go wrong this time?" Will it be the WiFi connection? Different versions of the meeting platform? Screen sharing? Forgetting to share or not to share? Not knowing what participants are seeing? A whole host of things that serve to increase cortisol, that wonderful stress hormone. Read on for some smiles and solutions.

8A. CAMERA ON/OFF (4-min)

EARLY IN THE PANDEMIC, I joined an online community

for a Zoom meeting/webinar, and I was sharing a laptop log-in with my wife. We used the "change name" feature to indicate we were both there on one account, and then quickly (and embarrassingly) learned that we had joined an hour after the session had started. I wanted to eat a sandwich, so I thought we should be off screen.

Unfortunately, we clicked "hide self" rather than "stop video." The result, for those of you who don't know, is that we no longer saw ourselves in the little Zoom squares, but everyone else still could see us. I only learned this when, by chance, I opened the "chat" window and saw a private message to me from one of the other participants: "Bon appétit, Andrew!"

This was embarrassing. But not as bad as what this Spanish news anchor faced:

(https://www.the-sun.com/news/755792/news-anchor-caught-cheating-naked-woman-video-call/

While at-home video conferences proliferate, almost everyone has a "horror story" or two to share, begging the question: Is it better to turn your camera on or leave it off? And along with that question comes the one about proper attire for video conferences. So let's look at both issues today.

LIGHTS, Camera (?), Action!

EVEN IF VIDEO meetings mean we're all actors now, it's

not clear we either want to be or that we are ready to be on stage, especially for hours at a time. So some opt out, turning their cameras off during meetings. If that's your wish, remember my painful lesson: "Stop Video," not "Hide Self." Depending on the purpose of the video conference and your company policy, this may be a good option. However, if you are trying to get as close to a "real" meeting as possible, then, especially from the leader/facilitator point of view, you'll want your camera on. It's disconcerting to see a bunch of black boxes with white names across them, or just photos, interspersed with some people on video, and with some responding and others not.

I suggest you clarify the purpose of the video conference and break it into time slots, with cameras off during some parts and on during others. Remember, these high-intensity video interactions are stressful for even the most extroverted among us. And just as closing your eyes may help you focus on content, "camera off" can have a similar effect. But again, if your aim is to recreate a lively, interactive meeting or to simulate a classroom (if you're a teacher or trainer) the best policy I've found is the one recommended by Hitotsubashi's School of International Corporate Strategy: "Cameras on." Just remember to include breaks with "cameras off." Have you noticed the drop in tension that comes from knowing the camera is off?

. . .

Dress Code?

Buzzing around the 'net are complaints and observations from all sides on this issue: How should you dress for a virtual meeting conducted from home? Some professionals are sticking to their work dress code, and bristle when colleagues aren't taking the time or making the effort to do the same. "They're being paid, they should at least look professional," wrote a corporate board member. Another company leader echoes this and requires his employees to "wear their battle fatigues." Yet the other side responds, "Look! We're in the middle of a pandemic, I'm watching two kids at home all day *and* trying to work, and now you're going to tell me I need to care about how I dress for a meeting? Forget that!"

All these arguments have their merit. I'd say that if your boss is the board member above, better to shower, groom, and suit up. Some add, "At least from the waist up," but I disagree. First of all, you may, for any number of reasons, need to suddenly stand up, and may, like me or that Casanova above, fail to turn off your video. Second, if you are dressing the part in order to convey a professional presence, don't split yourself in two. Your counterparts may not know that you're wearing shorts, but you do. But perhaps that's just me. You make the call!

If your boss shows up to video conferences wearing a hoodie or t-shirt, you may want to show up casual. (I was going to say, "You may want to follow suit," but I guess it would be more correct to say, "follow not suit.") And you may get a mix: The other day, the Daily Show's Trevor Noah was dressed in his patented hoodie-look while interviewing the dark-suited, white-shirted, blue-tied governor of New York. That may become common place, but until it does, I prefer a common code for a given team.

Longing for a New (and Better) Normal

STRANGE TIMES INDEED. Who would have thought we'd be throwing about words like "asymptomatic," "Zoom bombing," and "shelter-in-place?" Or that in the spring of 2020 we'd be reading about people drinking Lysol® or Clorox® to protect them from a virus? Yes, it actually happened. And as much as I want to "get back to normal," or, hopefully, to a "better normal," we will all be attending and leading more video conferences as time goes on. So we might as well learn as much as we can about how to perform better on them.

And who's to say these video conferences are any worse than one of the alternatives being floated, namely students and workshop participants all wearing masks? In Tokyo, during allergy season, we'd often see one or two of a given group wearing a mask, and believe me, it's hard to tell if they are getting the message or just wanting to get out of the room.

"It's not the strongest or most intelligent who will survive, but those who can best adapt to change." This cleaned up paraphrasing of Leon Meggison's summary of Charles Darwin's theory (yes, that's the pathway back to the meme's origin) provides me with inspiration and hope. Yes, there are challenges and embarrassments with new technology as we're exploring new ways of working and communicating. But if we keep adapting, we're much more likely to survive, and even thrive. "Lights, camera...ACTION!"

8B. CAMARA ON/OFF (2-min)

EARLY IN THE PANDEMIC, I joined a Zoom webinar, sharing a laptop with my wife. We had logged in an hour after the session had started, and I wanted to eat a sandwich, so I thought we should be off screen. Unfortunately, we clicked "hide self," not "stop video." The result? We couldn't see ourselves, but everyone else still could. How did I know? A private chat: "Bon appétit, Andrew!"

Embarrassing, yes. But not as bad as this Spanish news anchor:

https://www.the-sun.com/news/755792/news-anchor-caught-cheating-naked-woman-video-call.

Almost everyone has a "horror story" to share, begging the questions: Is it better to turn your camera off? And what about attire?

. . .

Lights, Camera (?), Action!

EVEN THOUGH WE'RE all actors now, some prefer not to be seen. If that's you, learn from my mistake and remember: "Stop Video," not "Hide Self." Depending on the meeting's purpose and your company's policy, this may work. However, if you're hoping to approximate a real meeting, you'll want everyone's camera on. It's odd to look at a screen of boxes, some with names, others with photos, and then some with people on live video.

Break longer meetings into "cameras on" and "cameras off" time slots. Remember, these high-intensity interactions are stressful for extroverts. And turning cameras off will help some people focus more on content. But if your aim is to foster a lively meeting or recreate an interactive classroom, I recommend "cameras on."

Dress Code?

SO MANY VIEWS ON ATTIRE! Some stick to their work dress code and bristle when colleagues don't. "They're being paid, they should at least look professional," wrote a board member. Another manager requires employees to "wear their battle fatigues." But then there's this: "Look! In the middle of a pandemic, two kids at home, I'm trying to get my work done, and now I need to dress up for a meeting too? Forget that!"

If my boss were that board member, I'd suit up. A friend adds, "At least above the waist," but what if you need to stand up? And if you're dressing to convey a professional presence, why split yourself in two? Your counterparts may not know that you're wearing shorts and sandals, but you and your subconscious do.

VIDEO CONFERENCING for the Long Run

WE ALL WANT to get back to normal, or to a "better normal," and guess what: That will include video meetings. So let's perform better on them.

And who's to say video meetings are any worse than co-workers, students and workshop participants all wearing masks? In Tokyo, during allergy season, we'd see one or two of a given group wearing a mask, and it's hard to tell if they are getting the message or just wanting to get out of the room.

"It's not the strongest or most intelligent who survive, but those who can best adapt to change." I'm inspired by that cleaned-up paraphrasing of Leon Meggison's summary of Sir Charles Darwin's famous theory. We're all dealing with challenges (and embarrassments) with new technology, with new ways of communicating. But if we keep adapting, we're much more likely to survive, and even thrive. So here we go: Lights...CameraS (that "S" means all cameras)... ACTION!

CHAPTER 8 COOL-DOWN NOTES

I'M WRITING this during the summer of 2020, in the midst of the worst global pandemic in 100 years. And as the Japanese might say, "fortunately and unfortunately" we didn't have modern technology back in 1918. Still, if you go through the news archives, you'll see there were controversies over mask-wearing, over business closings, even over voting, all eerily similar to today. What we have learned and haven't learned over the past century could both fill volumes.

Note again that this, as with all the other chapters, has managed to cover all we "need" to cover in half the words used for the original messaging. By reading both, and especially with the edited version second, the message will stick longer in your memory. And if you watched that sad Spanish newscaster video, you *will* remember to turn your camera off!

As a "Pot-shot®" postcard my mom gave me when I was a kid says, "I don't have a solution, but I certainly admire the problem." Simple solutions or not, it's up to us to navigate our way through these challenges. My blog is called *Andrew's Ax* for several reasons. One is that with a sharp ax, you can clear a path. You and your team can use the current situation (whatever "current" is right now) to discuss different solutions, and then experiment. My younger brother's Northwestern Wildcats football team (1995 and 1996 Big Ten champions) emblazoned a slogan on their practice t-shirts: "Either find a way or make a way." You and your team can too. Find or make a way that works best for you.

ZOOMICIDE?

I hope that through the first eight chapters of this little book you've discovered or rediscovered some useful tips, meaning some *actions* you can take to improve the quality of your remote work. And if you've read both versions of any of the chapters, you've also witnessed the benefit of being concise. Often, "less is more." This last chapter wraps up what we've covered and re-focuses directly on my purpose, the "Big Why," which could be expressed as "Zoomicide Prevention." We also dive into a few more hacks to raise your remote game.

9A. ZOOMICIDE? (4-min)

I DEBATED with myself over the title of this chapter. On the one hand, I don't want to make light of a very stressful time, and on the other hand, I absolutely *do* want to make light of just about everything. After all, "Angels can fly because they take themselves lightly."

Just as the summer 2020 world has been gripped by one story, the business communications world has also been captured by one subset of the story: How to work effectively online, with video-conferences replacing nearly all face-to-face meetings.

Early on in the pandemic, I presented for the American Chamber of Commerce in Japan's (ACCJ) "SME Roundtable," a weekly virtual event hosted by the SME CEO Council. This was my second ACCJ event on "virtually" the same topic, and it's the topic that dominates most of our coaching business as well. People are looking for help. And rightfully so!

Back to the Movies: The Good, the Bad, and the Ugly

If someone were to ask me to describe, in one word, my emotional state related to virtual meetings, I'd be torn between "Stressful" and "Mixed." I've enjoyed some very good sessions, including ones where I learned new tools discussed in this book (Polling, Breakout Groups, Mentimeter®, Kudobox®, Miro, Spatial Chat, to name a few), expertly facilitated and enjoyable throughout. Those "good" sessions have been entertaining and useful. Sadly, they make up no more than 20% of the sessions I've attended. The "bad" include those promoted as one thing (such as a "webinar") but that deliver something altogether different (often, an advertisement).

And then there's the "ugly." These are simply extensions of just about all the "ugly" things we see during physical meetings and presentations: Slides that can't be read (or are long and read aloud by the presenter); lack of interaction or engagement; all the elements best summed up as "lack of good communication or presentation skills." Some examples include poor vocal quality, filler word over-use, zero eye contact, poor posture. By now we all know the list.

I didn't want to wow ACCJ members with amazing visuals, since the session was a "large meeting." It wasn't a webinar (that really do call for slides)—it wasn't a "small meeting" where everyone's microphones are unmuted for constant interaction. Rather, it was a "large meeting" that I still wanted to be as interactive and useful as can reasonably be, given the "virtual" limitations.

How to Raise the Quality of Online Meetings

I HAD ONE AIM: Raise the quality of online meetings. Why? Because I attend them, and I'm sick 'n' tired of bad ones!

Some of my experiences online during these times

must match yours: When I've led them, they're stressful, taking up at least 3X more of my energy than in-person meetings or presentations. And yet, some have been super productive, especially when compared with the alternative: Zero contact. A mixed bag and none problem-free. The *New Yorker* once published a cartoon that showed two business colleagues talking across a desk, with one colleague saying, "You should be happy you have problems. The people without problems are dead."

One "problem" I was asked to address was "How can I increase engagement," so I shared a few ways. For small groups, act as a *facilitator* and make sure to call on quieter people. For medium-sized groups, use polling, chat, Q & A options, and physical expressions (get those on camera to give thumbs up or down, for example). For small and large groups alike, I suggested using the break-out function, with four caveats: 1) always give enough material for a break-out group to use so they don't finish way ahead of others with nothing to do; 2) let groups know they may not have enough time to finish; 3) inform them that they can request to come back to the main room or invite the facilitator into their breakout; 4) choose when and for how long to join breakout rooms yourself.

I shared with them something I wrote in an earlier chapter, and it's worth repeating: Unless you are a professional podcaster like Joe Rogan, or radio DJ who can keep an audience's attention without a guest, don't speak for more than 10 minutes on a video conference without some kind of **real** interaction. Even 10 minutes may be too long. And give a break every 30 minutes or so...many more breaks than a real meeting requires.

That's most of what I covered. There were lots of questions, and one participant made his own mini-speech, but even that was welcomed, because it was **another** voice (plus he offered some great advice). In the end, the organizer gave me some private feedback and said I came across "not as positive as usual," and that I too often bemoaned the use of WebEx compared with Zoom. He's right—I used more vinegar than sugar on that day, but I (and many others) are sick of bad video conferences. And for good reasons we prefer Zoom! In any case, I welcomed and appreciated the feedback. It's one more perspective.

Another ACCJ leader texted me during one of those "bad, ugly" web-based meetings, as we watched over a hundred on the call dwindle down to the 40s, then 30s: "That's a low number, and the ones who are left must be dead on the screen."

The title track of the movie *M.A.S.H.* is *Suicide is Painless*. I love the song but hate the lyrics, and am glad the TV series used an instrumental version. Because remember: "Zoomicide" is anything but painless.

9B. ZOOMICIDE PREVENTION (2-min)

I STRUGGLED with this chapter's title. I don't want to

make light of a stressful time, and yet I *do* want to make light of just about everything. After all, "Angels can fly because they take themselves lightly."

Business leaders today are asking, "How can we perform better on video conferences?" Recently I presented for the American Chamber of Commerce in Japan's (ACCJ) "SME Roundtable," a virtual event hosted by the SME CEO Council. This was my second ACCJ event on the same topic. People are looking for help. Here's some:

Back to the Movies: The Good, the Bad, and the Ugly

If you ask me to describe my feelings re: "Virtual Meetings," I'm torn between "Stressful" and "Mixed." I've enjoyed some good sessions. I've learned new tools (Polling, Breakout Groups, Mentimeter®, and Spatial Chat to name three). Good sessions. Entertaining and useful. Sadly, they make up about 20% of those I've attended. The bad include "webinars" that are really advertisements and sessions with tech troubles.

And then there's the *ugly*, extensions of all the ugly that we see in physical meetings: Unreadable slides, lack of engagement. Elements summed up as lack of good presentation skills, including: poor vocal quality, filler words ("you know"), zero eye contact, poor posture. You know the list. Add in "failure to mute and unmute properly" and it's often an ugly ride.

Raising the Quality of Online Meetings

At the ACCJ session, I had one aim: Raise the quality of online meetings. We're tired of bad and ugly ones! How do my experiences online during these times compare with yours? As a leader, they take 3X more energy than regular meetings. And yet, some have been super productive, especially when compared with the alternative: No contact.

A participant asked, "How can I increase engagement?" Answer: For small groups, act as a *facilitator* and directly call on quieter people. For medium-sized groups, use polling, chat, Q & A buttons, and physical expressions (thumbs up or down, for example). For small and large groups alike, I use the break-out function, with three caveats: 1) have enough material for a group to use, 2) let groups know they may not have enough time to finish, and that they can come back to the main room or invite me into their breakout; 3) choose when and for how long to join breakout rooms yourself.

Again: Unless you're a podcaster like Joe Rogan who can keep an audience's attention without a guest, don't speak for more than 10 minutes on a video conference without *real* interaction. Even 10 minutes may be too long. And take breaks every 30 minutes. Cameras off, stand up and exercise! Push-ups, Jumping Jacks, whatever!

That's most of what I covered. There were lots of questions, and one participant made his own mini-speech, but even that was welcomed because it was *another* voice (and he offered some good advice).

One leader recently texted me, as we watched over 100 on a call dwindle down to the mid-40s, then 30s: "That's low, and the ones who are left are dead on the screen," he wrote.

The title track of the movie *M.A.S.H.* is *Suicide is Painless*. I love the song but hate the lyrics, and I'm glad the TV series used an instrumental version. Let's strive for better performance because "Zoomicide" is anything but painless.

CHAPTER 9 COOL-DOWN NOTES

THIS TIME, the editing process led me to change the title of the chapter. My primary purpose in this book is to help you enjoy remote work, and web-based meetings more. So I came right out and said it: It's all about "Zoomicide Prevention." Sometimes editors will recommend you cut out anything "cute," but I really like the idea of preventing Zoomicide, so it stays. That's part of the beauty of 2020: We can skip right past many the gatekeepers of days gone by.

They say a cat has nine lives, and this book has nine chapters. If your next remote meeting goes badly, treat it as one more "life," knowing you can get back up, share your experience, and focus on making the next meeting better. I have yet to attend an outside-led virtual meeting that ends with a simple survey, one we've used for years at AMT Group: "What went well? What can we do to improve our next meeting?" Two simple questions that can self-guide your team toward better, more productive meetings. How about experimenting with that as a way to end your next meeting?

Like with everything else, "good and bad" comes along for the ride with remote work. Some have found *more* time as they can skip a long commute. Others lament the distractions at home or other remote set-ups. Some have been able to gladly take on more work; others feel the burden of higher expectations. As of the summer 2020, I'm still waiting for the salesperson who reports that she or he is closing *more* deals without face-to-face visits, but even sales activities are moving more online.

Summer is a time of graduations, of what they call "Commencements," which, as a recent Hitotsubashi alumni reminded the ICS MBA class of 2020, "means a beginning." In that spirit, let this chapter's "cool-down notes" serve as a "warm-up" for your next remote work session, beginning with a *Remote Work Charter*, something like:

· · ·

When in the course of human events it becomes necessary for us to work remotely at least some of the time, be it resolved that we will do our best to:

1. *Be prepared—with our computers, work spaces, camera, lighting.*
2. *Avoid distractions.*
3. *Be clear and concise.*
4. *Be open to technology that improves our work.*
5. *Recognize that challenges do not hit all of us equally.*
6. *Create shared norms and expectations for what work is done remotely, in person, or both.*
7. *LISTEN.*
8. *LAUGH.*

WE DIDN'T COVER number 8 in this book. Maybe someday I'll write *Get a G.R.I.P. on Humor*. But if there's one thing that's hard to write, it's to write funny. I *can* tell you, though, that my best calls, and my best work, get done with a spirit of fun. When the leader has a good sense of humor, and lets people know it's OK to mess up, all the better.

As an example, for the 2020 ICS commencement, we professors received three separate e-mails reminding us to install the newest version of Zoom and to follow certain protocols. Despite this, a couple professors didn't follow the requirements. But because the leader also asked us to call in early, he was able to help those profs get set up. And there was no reprimanding, no impatient, "Didn't you get the message?" None of that. Good humor won the day.

So, as we close this chapter, wherever it is in your reading (maybe you came here first), have you set up your space? Established your positive mindset? Is your technology up to speed, with a stable internet connection? Can you sign on to the *Charter* suggested? Recall the issues we covered in this book so that you can turn *The Good, the Bad, and the Ugly* into *Good, Better Best*? My dad used a short poem to drill in those comparatives, and I'd like to use it as a motivator for all of our remote work, through and beyond the pandemic:

Good, Better, Best

Good, better, best
Never let it rest
'till your good is better
And your better BEST

MAY your good remote work get better, and your better remote work approach the very BEST.

REMOTE BALANCE

Early draft readers of *Get a G.R.I.P. on Remote Work* suggested I tackle a 40,000-foot question I'd ignored or glossed over. Voilá! A Bonus Chapter (just one three-minute read) on *Balance*.

I won a VLUV balance ball at a charity event, and I've enjoyed using it as my desk chair ever since our move this summer. It took a little getting used to, and feels a bit like exercise, but who doesn't need more exercise? So thanks to Karl Hahne and Hafele Japan for turning me on to this modern office addition.

I'd used balance balls for workouts in the past, and "Balance" is one of AMT Group's Action Values (the others being Creativity, Empowering, Encouraging, and Listening), so it's only fitting that I address the topic of "balance" in the context of remote work. Fitting, and requested (as mentioned above) by a few readers. The readers shared how the pandemic has wreaked havoc on their balance, with challenges popping up everywhere: at home, at work, and those "third spaces" like Starbucks.

Since the New Normal that's coming will contain a mix of working at home, working at clients' offices, and logging in from temporary work spaces along with the traditional in-person collaboration, how will you manage all this? Each reader will have his or her own way, and I encourage experimenting. First, as I suggested in Chapter 1, find your *chronotype* and match work activities to your type as much as you can.

Here's how it has been shaping up for me: I take care of creative, solitary work like writing at home, at a coffee shop, or at a collaborative work space, usually in the mid-morning hours. There are several inexpensive "WeWork-type" alternatives in Tokyo. Some cost less than $10 a day, require no membership fees, and their daily rate includes beverages, WiFi and copy services. What options do you have around you?

To deliver online coaching or group seminars, I prefer a consistent set-up where I know the lighting will be good, WiFi stable, and where I can quickly access hard copies I may need. So for those, I use my home office.

The New Normal brings a question to nearly everyone: How often and for what purposes will you go into the office? This is one of those areas where *equity*, rather than *equality* should rule the day. My hope is that organizations would seek to treat everyone equitably—that is, "fairly and impartially," which is not the same as treating everyone "equally." If some on your team do their best work remotely, why require them to come in more than is absolutely necessary? And why not offer those who thrive in an office environment more face-time? (Not Apple's app, but real face-time!)

It's long been recommended that emotional issues be solved face-to-face rather than over text or e-mail. I've seen minor misunderstandings over a simple word like "apparently" lead to major conflicts and "flame-wars" when having people sit in the same room would have avoided the misunderstanding, or at least would have allowed it to be cleared up in a matter of minutes. I also am a firm believer in regular catch-up, feedback, or coaching/mentoring meetings, so that subordinates know they will have a set time during which they can bring up any issue with their boss. For those regular meetings, as regular cadence of, say, once every two weeks makes sense to me.

WORK-LIFE ALEX?

SEVERAL YEARS AGO, we were assessing a team on their Global Readiness®, and one of the elements the team leader wanted to improve was "work-life balance." He told us, "I'm not even sure how many of my (all Japanese) staff are familiar with the term." Boy, was he right! During one of the first interviews, we asked a team member, "How would you describe your work-life balance?" He replied, "Work-life Alex?"

We laughed at the time, but early in the pandemic, when the days and even weeks rolled into each other, it seemed that work-life balance got sheltered-in-place, and completely out of sight, perhaps with Alex. Now, with "work from home" more common, finding balance is even harder. As late as September 2020 one commenter from San Francisco wrote, "I finish work and I'm still home. Then I'm home but still at work. I don't like it." Some may not like it, but there's a lot you can do to make it better, for yourself and for those like that San Francisco commenter.

The "new normal" will see more innovative ways in which "non-quantifiable" work will be measured, so that more of us are paid for output rather than for hours logged. This may create less steady income for those who relied on regular wages, but to me, that's preferable to micromanaging time spent in front of a computer that some companies engage in.

At the dawn of the Knowledge Age, visionary futurists like John Naisbitt (author of *Megatrends* and seven other books) told us to focus on the invisible (services, digital information), on the small players rather than the giant corporations, and, later, to keep our eyes on the growing influence of China. Who would have known, back in the early 1980s, other than Naisbitt and maybe Dean Koontz, that an invisible virus from China would accelerate our journey away from tradition and into the wilds of remote work?

I am using that balance ball as a desk chair, while other leaders are going further, working while standing or exercising. One recent podcast guest was being interviewed while walking on his treadmill. What used to be metaphorically synonymous with drudgery has become a norm for some. These people are *literally* working on a treadmill! What's next, "noses to the grindstone?"

Remote work is a mixed blessing, an opportunity and a challenge for different people in different ways. Individuals and organizations with agility—those having developed, practiced, and rewarded **balance**—are the ones who are going to do more than just survive in the New Normal. I trust with your better G.R.I.P. on remote work, you will be among those who thrive.

IF YOU ENJOYED THIS BOOK...

If you enjoyed this book, please consider subscribing to our mailing list at www.amt-group.com. Reviews are great assistance. If you liked the book, please consider leaving your thoughts in the review section of the online retailer where you made the purchase.

ABOUT THE AUTHOR

Andrew Silberman has been inspiring improvement in individuals and organizations since 1989. At AMT Group, which he co-founded in Tokyo in 1992, he leads a multi-national team of facilitators and administrative staff whose mission is: *Developing Global Thinkers*.

Andrew was born in Chicago, Illinois, and lived his primary through high school years in Saratoga, California. He holds a bachelor's degree in the Political Economy of Industrial Societies from U.C. Berkeley and graduated (with distinction) with an MBA in international management from the Fisher School of Business at the Monterey Institute of International Studies.

Made in the USA
Coppell, TX
29 October 2020

40426347R00059